The
World of
Mexican Cooking

The World of Mexican Cooking

MARY MARGARET CURRY

ILLUSTRATED BY BETTY STIFF

GALAHAD BOOKS • NEW YORK CITY

Contents

Refried Beans
Preparation of Tortillas

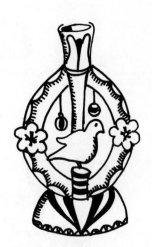

The
World of
Mexican Cooking

A Note From The Author

Women in their roles of wives, mothers, and cooks are so often thwarted by the endless tasks which consume their hours and dull their senses that they feel somewhat dehumanized and intellectually stunted. As a result, they often build up resentments which lead to unhappiness with their way of life.

Individuals often do not realize that they can find a release from the pressures of daily living by involving themselves in some form of creative work. Until they have found an outlet, they have no conception of the happiness and feeling of accomplishment that will be theirs. Women, after they have been released from the early bondage of baby bottles and diapers, do have a certain amount of time to devote to creative projects within their homes. They can turn to refinishing furniture, upholstering, making slip-covers, drapes, bedspreads, or dressmaking; but, above all, they can spend happy days, weeks, and months mastering the art of cooking.

Cooking can be tedious, boring and frustrating, but only if it is approached with that attitude. All women will at times get into a rut where they find themselves cooking the same thing week after week and, of course, receiving no bouquets for the monotony of their menus. However, they have only to pick up a good cookbook, read a few recipes, and they will find their imagination sparked.

It is admitted that very few wives and mothers have the time or energy to turn out a masterpiece a day, but to do it even once a week would be quite an accomplishment, and the sweetest moment of all is when you serve a really great meal to guests and they sigh with enjoyment. It is then worth the many hours you may have spent in preparation of the meal.

This is a cookbook of Mexican food as it is cooked in South Texas. These recipes were at one time of Mexican origin, and some still are. Most of them, however, have evolved into something that now has a Texas twist. I think of these Mexican dishes as being Tex-Mex, which is a bastardized form of Spanish spoken here in South Texas.

We consider our Mexican food unique and delicious. Texans who move away write back wistfully of the delights of yesteryear. One joyful aspect of Mexican food is that it is relatively inexpensive to prepare. Also, once you learn some of the fundamentals of Mexican cooking, most of it is simply and quickly done. I know that you will love what we so happily eat here in South Texas and it will give a fillip to cooking. Have fun and, as Julia Child might say in Spanish, *¡come con gusto!*

The World of Mexican Cooking

DOS AND DON'TS AND IFS AND ANDS

As much as I use olive oil when cooking, I never use it for Mexican food. It does something to Mexican cooking that takes away its authenticity.

To my way of thinking, most food is never quite as good after it has been frozen (rice, for example, becomes mushy); but there are a few dishes that freeze beautifully. Offhand, I can think of three: enchilada sauce, chili con carne, and pinto beans covered with their own juice. Any other dish that does well in the deep freeze will have a notation to that effect in the recipe.

Naturally, it will be great if you can buy all the ingredients called for in these recipes, but in certain parts of the United States they may not be available. If that is your problem, start searching the canned goods counters, and if there are specialty stores selling foreign foods, all the better. The following ingredients or foods are readily obtainable in cans, bottles or jars almost everywhere: tamales, chili con carne, tortillas, chili powder, Chiliquik, cumin, chiles serranos, chiles poblanos (called green chilies on can), cooked Mexican rice, hot sauce, enchilada sauce (some brands are far superior), chili con queso, and crisp tortilla triangles. Of course, the canned foods cannot compare with the home-cooked product, but if you're hooked on Mexican food, you'll welcome them nevertheless.

Now that we are so cholesterol conscious I suppose I shouldn't mention it, but authentic Mexican cooking includes the use of pure lard. I don't use it except when making up the masa for tamales or tortillas. I have been brainwashed to the extent that I am convinced the tamales wouldn't be good without lard.

CHILI PEPPERS AND THEIR USES

At this point, we must form a study group and discuss the chile pepper. There are several kinds and they have varying uses. Three of them are used for their pepper-hot quality. These are chiles serranos, a small bright green pepper, about one and a half inches long; the chile petine, which is pure fire; and the jalapeño, which is no slouch in vying for the nomination to King Fire Pepper. I have friends who use fresh jalapeños purchased here in San Antonio, home base for this book, but I have never used them. I buy the canned ones.

Chile pods, or chiles pisados, are next in line for consideration. These are dark red to almost black and, because they have been dried, they are wizened in appearance. Chile pods are used for making enchilada sauce and chili, if you wish to do it the hard way since chili powder can be used just as well. At this point I will be accused of heresy or—worse yet—of being a rotten cook, by the small band of purists. Bloodied but unbowed, I stand my ground.

Finally, we come to the peppers used for chiles rellenos. First, let us get the bell pepper out of the way. It is the least desirable of all peppers for this dish, mainly because of its overpowering green pepper taste. If it is the only one available, it can be used, but it must first be boiled in water before using until somewhat tender.

The ideal pepper is chile poblano, a wide, flat, dark green pepper. It has a delicate flavor, provided you remove all the seeds which are hot, hot, hot. Happily, you can buy them canned and they have been roasted and peeled. On the can they are called green chilies.

The Anaheim pepper, which I understand many local Mexican restaurants use for chiles rellenos, is very long, flat and bright green.

FLOUR AND MORE FLOUR

In cooking Mexican food there are two kinds of flour used: wheat flour, found in everyone's kitchen, and corn flour, made from corn and called masa. Masa, a moist mixture, is very perishable, so it should be used the same day it is purchased or it might sour. It can be obtained at a molino, a specialty store found only in areas of a city inhabited by Mexican-Americans. Luckily there is now a product on the market called masa harina, a dry masa you mix with water. Since masa is not readily obtainable, this is a boon to Mexican cooking.

Basic
Recipes

It is necessary that you know these basic recipes which you will need for the preparation of various Mexican dishes.

HOT SAUCE

Here in Southwest Texas, hot sauce is spooned over almost every type of Mexican food. In Mexican restaurants there is always a bowl of it served with your order whether you want it or not. It can range from mild to liquid fire. We are most happy when the tears are streaming down our cheeks—that means a successful hot sauce. To reduce the tears, reduce the number of chile peppers. Remember, the seeds are the hottest part of the pepper.

> *4 chiles serranos*
> *1 clove garlic*
> *1 tablespoon cooking oil*
> *1 can (14 ½ oz.) tomatoes*
> *½ teaspoon salt*

Chop fine chiles serranos and the garlic clove. Sauté a few minutes in about one tablespoon cooking oil and add tomatoes, broken up. Add salt and simmer about five minutes. Serve cold.

GUACAMOLE

At one time, I put everything I could find in guacamole, and it was good, but the delicate flavor of the avocado was lost. Now I make it with lemon juice and salt only and like it even more.

> *3 medium ripe avocados*
> *1 ¼ teaspoon salt*
> *1 small tomato (optional)*
> *Juice of 2 lemons*

Cut avocados in half, remove seeds (save them) and, with a spoon, scoop avocado out of shell into bowl. The avocado can be put through a food mill but it is even better to mash it with a fork. Please don't put it in your blender—it just doesn't taste right.

Add lemon juice and salt, mix well, and taste. If it is not "lemony" enough, add more lemon juice and be sure it has enough salt to give it character. You can, if you like, add one small tomato, chopped fine; and my daughter insists it have Tabasco sauce. You can even add crushed garlic, finely grated onion, and chiles serranos or jalapeños, chopped very fine, but please don't add cream, cream cheese or mayonnaise. It simply won't be guacamole.

You have carefully saved the seeds, I hope. Put them in the bowl of guacamole. It's supposed to keep the avocado from turning color and is picturesque.

PINTO BEANS

This is so simple to make that it seems ridiculous to write a recipe for it, and yet there are a few dos and don'ts. Some people seem to think that beans have to be cooked all day. Why? I don't know. In four hours I can have the finished product.

First, you simply must use pinto beans. It just isn't a Mexican dish if you don't. They do not have to be soaked overnight.

1 lb. pinto beans
12 cups cold water
1 large onion, cut into eighths
3 cloves garlic, crushed
2 ½ to 3 teaspoons salt
4 tablespoons bacon drippings

Wash beans thoroughly and remove rocks so that you will not have a broken tooth. In a large pot, put the beans in water, bring to a boil, and then turn the fire low. Add onion, garlic, salt, and bacon drippings, and cook until beans are tender. When skins are broken and beans mash easily, they are done. They really should be cooked four hours. During the cooking time, if liquid boils down too low, add some boiling water. The finished dish should be on the soupy side. Some of these beans inside a folded over flour tortilla is a fine treat. Oh, yes, they freeze beautifully if they are covered with their own juice.

REFRIED BEANS

Drain cooked beans, put in frying pan with very hot (but not smoking) bacon drippings and mash with a potato masher. Cook until grease is absorbed and beans are rather crusty on bottom of pan. After they are cooked, you may put a little grated cheese atop the beans. Hot sauce really gives them a punch.

In restaurants they are often served with crisp tortilla triangles stuck into the beans. Serve with almost anything, but they are a must with huevos rancheros.

PREPARATION OF TORTILLAS

So many of the recipes in this book call for tortillas that it is best you know how to prepare them in advance. Tortillas are used either crisp or "soft."

Soft Tortilla

In a small frying pan, immerse tortilla in one-half inch of hot (but not smoking) cooking oil for about thirty seconds, turning once and then immediately removing to plate with food turner. Tortilla must not get crisp but must remain pliable so that it can be easily rolled up.

Crisp Tortilla

In a small frying pan, immerse tortilla in one-half inch of hot (but not smoking) cooking oil until it becomes crisp. During the cooking time, turn tortilla once or twice with food turner. Put on paper towel to drain. These are used in preparation of chalupas.

For tacos, tortillas are cooked as follows: in a small frying pan, immerse tortilla in about one inch of hot (but not smoking) cooking oil and, with the use of two tablespoons, immediately fold tortilla in half. With one spoon inserted between the taco sides, so there will be a space for the filling, and the other spoon holding the taco in position, fry until crisp, turning once. The tortilla, emerging as a taco shell, should resemble a narrow U when viewed from the side. After a little practice you will be an old pro.

To make nachos, or crisp tortilla triangles, quarter the tortillas and fry in hot oil until they are crisp. Remove with food turner and keep in warm oven until ready to serve or use for nachos.

Party
Foods

All of the recipes in this chapter are suitable for cocktail parties or for hors d'oeuvres. They're so tasty one must exercise self-restraint in order to leave room for the meal that follows.

MARGUERITAS

This is a drink that can be lethal, but I think this version is safe enough. I will never forget the dinner party I gave one time when I served Margueritas twice as strong as they should be—pure ignorance on my part—and we staggered into dinner. It was a most hilarious party and most interesting, but I have been careful not to repeat it.

1 can (5 ½ oz.) frozen lime juice, thawed
1 lime juice can of tequila
1 lime juice can ⅓ full of Triple Sec
Ice

Put lime juice, tequila and Triple Sec in blender. Finish filling with ice cubes, put top on, and turn on full speed until ice is pulverized. The noise is deafening but it only lasts about half a minute. Run half a lime around the rim of each glass and dip in salt. Pour Marguerita and serve. *¡Muy borracho!* You can safely serve two before dinner.

A blender-full can be made in advance and put in the deep freeze. Before serving, blend again for two or three seconds.

CHEESE NACHOS

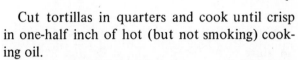

Tortillas
Cheddar cheese
Jalapeños
Cooking oil

Cut tortillas in quarters and cook until crisp in one-half inch of hot (but not smoking) cooking oil.

On a cookie sheet, arrange crisp tortilla triangles and on each one place a thin slice of cheese. Top with a small slice of jalapeño—it is very hot! and put under broiler until cheese is melted. Serve immediately.

Nachos with Beans and Cheese

Crisp tortilla triangles
Hot mashed pinto beans
Cheddar cheese
Jalapeños

Drain hot cooked pinto beans and mash with potato masher. Spread beans on tortilla triangles, top with thin slice of cheese and a slice of jalapeño. Put under broiler until cheese is melted. This is more hearty than the beanless nachos and could even be eaten with a salad as a light lunch.

There are a few brands of canned refried pinto beans which are acceptable and can be used in place of the home cooked beans. Test and taste.

EMPANADAS

Almost every country in the world has, I imagine, some form of the little pie. Some are baked, some are fried and everything imaginable is put inside of them. This is the Mexican-Texan version and they are greeted with delight by one and all. For coffees, brunches and cocktail parties with a Mexican theme they are excellent.

Any fruit filling can be used instead of pumpkin or sweet potato, but it would not be as Mexican in character. There is also the meat-filled empanada which is very Mexican. That recipe is given in another chapter. For the meat and cheese empanadas you would omit the sugar from the dough.

I have prepared as many as 150 empanadas in advance and frozen them. Place them on greased cookie sheets, cover with Saran Wrap and put in deep freeze. Unfreeze before baking. They're the same as fresh baked.

> *2 cups flour, sifted*
> *2 teaspoons baking powder*
> *½ teaspoon salt*
> *⅔ cups shortening*
> *¼ cup of sugar, dissolved in milk*
>   *used for dough*
> *About ½ teaspoon anise oil (optional)*
> *⅔ cup milk*

Sift dry ingredients together and cut in shortening. Add milk, sugar and anise oil and stir just
until dough follows fork around bowl. Knead
two or three times on floured board and roll out
about one-fourth inch thick. Cut in four-inch
circles. Now make your filling.

Pumpkin Empanadas

Filling:
1 can (16 oz.) pumpkin or mashed
  sweet potatoes
¾ cup sugar
About ½ teaspoon anise oil (optional)
1 teaspoon powdered allspice

Put all ingredients together and mix well.
Place one heaping teaspoon pumpkin or sweet
potato mixture on one half of the circle of
dough, fold over, and crimp edges with fork.
Brush pie with canned milk or egg white and
bake on greased cookie sheet at 450 degrees for
twelve to fifteen minutes or until pie is golden
brown. When baked, sprinkle with mixture of
sugar and cinnamon and serve warm.

Cheese Empanadas

Use same recipe for dough used in pumpkin empanadas, but omit sugar. Grate cheddar or American cheese, depending on which you like. Place about one heaping teaspoon on round of dough. Top with slice of jalapeño. Moisten edges of dough with egg white or condensed milk, fold over, crimp edges with fork, and bake on greased cookie sheet at 450 degrees for twelve to fifteen minutes or until pie is golden brown. It will brown better if you brush pie with condensed milk or egg white. Serve hot. Jalapeños are *hot*, so beware.

Shrimp Empanadas

Use same recipe for dough used in pumpkin empanadas, but omit sugar.

½ lb. raw shrimp, shelled and
   deveined and cut in very small pieces
⅓ cup butter
2 tablespoons lemon juice

Sauté cut up shrimp in melted butter and lemon juice until shrimp is cooked. This takes only two to three minutes. Place about one heaping teaspoon on round of dough. Fold over, crimp edges, and bake the same as for pumpkin empanadas. Omit sugar and cinnamon on pies. Serve hot.

GUACAMOLE DIP

See page 20 for the guacamole recipe. Serve this in bowl with accompanying Fritos or crisp tortilla triangles for dipping.

FLAQUITOS

See page 41 for recipe, the only difference being that you cut the tortilla in half before preparing flaquitos so that they will be bite size. Serve with guacamole. They can be used for dipping instead of Fritos or tortillas.

BEAN DIPS

Bean dips are great for teenage parties. The following recipe makes a heap of dip and this is good, because having a group of teenagers is like inviting a horde of locusts.

Bean and Cheese Dip

1 lb. pinto beans, cooked
4 tablespoons bacon drippings
1 onion, chopped finely
2 cloves garlic, crushed
½ lb. cheddar cheese, grated
Jalapeños

Cook beans according to recipe on page 22. While still hot, pour off liquid, reserving some in the event the dip needs moistening. Mash beans well with potato masher. Set aside.

In large frying pan, sauté onion and garlic in about four tablespoons bacon drippings until onion is clear. Add mashed beans and mix well. Cook over low fire for about ten minutes, stirring occasionally, until mixture is hot. Add grated cheese and some chopped jalapeños, making it as hot as you like it. Serve in chafing dish and have a bowl of crisp tortilla triangles nearby to dip into the bean dip.

Bean and Chorizo Dip

This is made like regular bean and cheese dip except that you add about one pound of chorizo—Mexican sausage—which has been fried and drained of excess grease. You may omit the cheese if you wish. Chorizo comes in bulk and in links. If you buy the links, you would, of course, remove the casings before frying the meat.

CHILE CON QUESO

For many years I made various chile con quesos and was never satisfied with them. Few restaurants do well with this dish either. My main complaint is that it is generally too ropey. Finally a friend gave me this recipe, and I have been delighted with it.

2 scallions, minced
2 tablespoons cooking oil
1 medium tomato (¼ lb.)
4 chiles serranos
½ teaspoon salt
¼ small onion
¾ lb. American cheese, cut in small chunks
1 egg, slightly beaten

Spear tomato with fork and hold over fire until skin pops and curls. Remove skin. Put whole tomato, chiles serranos, one quarter onion and salt in water to cover and boil ten minutes. Remove tomato, chiles and pieces of onion from water and grind in molcajete or put through food mill. Set aside. Save one-third cup of the water.

Sauté scallions in two tablespoons cooking oil until they begin to brown. Remove excess oil and add tomato mixture and cheese and heat over very low fire. As cheese begins to melt, slowly add water, stirring constantly. When all water has been added and cheese is completely melted, add egg, continuing to stir, and cook about three or four minutes. Serve immediately in chafing dish with crisp tortilla triangles nearby for dipping purposes.

The Crispy, Crunchy Side of Tortillas

TACOS

If a poll were taken, tacos might be tops on the list for Mexican foods, but others would say enchiladas, and still others chalupas, and on it goes ad infinitum. Personally, I like all Mexican food and would be hard put to it to have to make a choice.

Tacos are crunchy morsels and can be filled with almost everything. Good table manners and taco eating are incompatible. The first bite disintegrates the taco, or part of it, and you will find that they have to be eaten in a low crouch over the plate. All tacos have a filling and are topped with chopped up lettuce and tomatoes plus a little hot sauce. The taco meat can be frozen for about two weeks.

Meat Tacos

1 lb. ground beef
½ medium onion, chopped fine
1 clove garlic, mashed
1 teaspoon cumin, ground
1 teaspoon salt
Pepper to taste
1 small tomato, chopped fine
10 tortillas
Shredded lettuce

Prepare ten taco shells (see page 23) and keep in warm place.

In large frying pan (do not use any cooking oil), crumble ground meat, preferably chuck, and cook over a high fire, breaking up meat with fork, until meat has lost its color and almost all liquid has cooked away. Do not brown meat. Add onion, garlic, cumin, salt and pepper. Sauté until onion turns clear. Add tomato and about two tablespoons water. Cover and cook over very low flame for about twenty minutes. When the meat is cooked, it should be quite moist. To achieve this result, you may have to add a little more water during the cooking time.

While the meat is cooking, chop enough tomatoes and lettuce (separately) so that you will have enough to top the filling in ten tacos.

Tacos should not be assembled until immediately before serving, as the moisture in the meat will make the taco shell soggy. With a slotted spoon, put two or three heaping tablespoons of meat in each taco shell and about one tablespoon lettuce and one tablespoon tomatoes on top of meat. Serve immediately. Hot sauce optional.

Chicken Tacos

1 small fryer or 3 chicken breasts
1 stalk of celery
1 bay leaf
1 teaspoon salt

Simmer chicken with celery, bay leaf, and salt until chicken is done. Remove chicken from broth (save broth and freeze, as it has many uses) and remove bones and skins. Shred chicken into very small pieces. Add a few spoons of broth to shredded chicken so that it is moist. Put in warming oven or other warm place. Any chicken left over after making tacos can be used for salads, etc.

Follow procedure outlined in meat tacos recipe, using lettuce and tomatoes for topping.

Chicken Tacos Compuestos

Prepare chicken tacos and top filling with guacamole.

Guacamole Tacos

In crisp taco shells put generous helping of guacamole (see page 20). Lettuce and tomato topping is optional. Hot sauce goes wonderfully with these. Serve immediately.

Avocado Tacos

This is the same as guacamole tacos except that you use slices of avocado instead. You can go wild and add chicken to the avocados. It is really good.

Sour Cream Chicken Tacos

Cooked chicken breasts, sliced
Sliced avocado
Salt
Tortillas, crisp or soft
Sour cream

If you use soft tortillas, remember to immerse them for thirty seconds in hot grease, being careful not to let them become crisp.

Place sliced chicken and avocado on crisp tortilla (if using soft, roll up tortilla after chicken and avocado are on it), salt to taste, and top with sour cream. Makes an appetizing luncheon dish.

CHALUPAS

Chalupas are a flattened-out version of tacos and are equally good. You start out by making a "crisp tortilla," allowing two to a serving.

Bean Chalupas

Cook pinto beans (see page 22), and you might as well cook one pound while you're at it since they freeze so well. Drain the hot cooked beans you plan to use, allowing about four heaping tablespoons of beans for each tortilla, and mash with a potato masher. With a knife, spread hot beans over crisp tortilla and sprinkle generously with grated cheddar cheese. Put chalupas on cookie sheet and place under broiler until cheese is thoroughly melted. Serve immediately topped with the usual chopped lettuce and tomatoes. Hot sauce optional.

Chalupas Compuestas

Prepare bean chalupas and serve topped with guacamole about one inch high, instead of the chopped lettuce and tomatoes. A dish fit for a king!

Double Decker Chalupas

Using a crisp tortilla, cover with cooked, shredded chicken, then a layer of guacamole, then a layer of sour cream, and top with another crisp tortilla. One of these is generally a meal unless you're a hearty eater.

FLAQUITOS

This is good for a luncheon, or it can be served for dinner along with other dishes. You will need chicken, celery, bay leaf, and tortillas. I am not giving amounts because it all depends on how many guests you have, and you simply add to or decrease the amounts of chicken and number of tortillas.

Simmer chicken in salted water with celery and bay leaf until done. Remove from broth and remove skin and bones. Shred chicken very fine. Keep warm while preparing tortillas.

Immerse tortilla in one-half inch of hot (but not smoking) cooking oil for thirty seconds, turning once. Tortilla must not get crisp and must remain pliable. Place about one heaping tablespoon chicken left of center of tortilla, roll up tightly so that it resembles a skinny cigar, and run two round toothpicks through the ends. Make several of these for each serving. Cook in fairly deep hot fat until they are crisp, turning once during cooking period, and remove to paper towels to drain. Remove toothpicks— which is not too easy. I have at times resorted to pliers. Serve flaquitos while hot with a glob of guacamole on each plate.

The Other Side of the Coin— Soft Tortillas

SOFT TACOS

These are entirely different from crisp tacos. They are served with a thick tomato sauce and can be topped with a dollop of sour cream if you wish.

Prepare ten soft tacos (see page 23), Prepare chicken or meat according to recipe for tacos (see pages 36 and 37). Make the following tomato sauce:

½ medium onion, chopped
1 clove garlic, crushed
1 tablespoon cooking oil
1 can (14½ oz.) tomatoes, broken
   into small pieces
½ teaspoon salt

Sauté onion and garlic in one tablespoon cooking oil until onion is clear. Add tomatoes and salt. Simmer about ten minutes.

Put about two heaping tablespoons chicken or meat mixture along center of tortilla, roll up cigar fashion, and use two to a serving. Spoon some of the hot tomato sauce on top of each serving and add some sour cream if you wish. Be sure everything, including the serving plates, is warm before assembling tacos, and serve immediately.

This would be nice served with a dish of guacamole into which crisp tortilla triangles are stuck.

Another good combination is soft tacos topped with a generous helping of guacamole. Omit tomato sauce.

FRIED CHEESE TACOS

2 cups masa harina
1⅛ cups water
Grated cheddar cheese
Jalapeño, sliced
1 teaspoon salt
2 tablespoons melted lard or cooking oil

Stir salt into masa harina and add water and melted shortening. Knead until well blended. Roll into small balls (this amount makes from ten to twelve). Place ball of dough between two pieces of waxed paper and roll into circle of about three to four inches. On this circle of dough, put some grated cheese and a slice of jalapeño. Fold over dough, making a half pie, and pinch edges together with a fork. Fry in hot fat, turning once, until golden brown and eat while hot. Makes me hungry just to write this one.

BEAN ROLLS

Immerse tortilla in one-half inch cooking oil, hot but not smoking, for thirty seconds, turning once. Remove immediately with food turner. Put one tablespoon refried beans along center of tortilla and roll up. Serve warm with hot sauce.

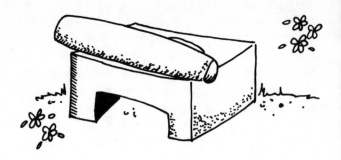

FLOUR TORTILLAS

Flour tortillas have always been eaten by South Texans of Mexican ancestry and by other Texans in rural areas, but I have noticed that during the past ten years the city dwellers have discovered flour tortillas and all that goes with them. They are quite easy to make, but rolling them out in perfect circles is something else again, at least for me. My husband never ceases to be amused and amazed by my square tortillas.

2 cups sifted flour
4 tablespoons shortening or
  pure lard, chilled
1½ teaspoons salt
1 teaspoon baking powder
⅔ cup warm water

Sift flour, salt and baking powder and cut in shortening as you do for pie crusts. Slowly add warm water as you blend all ingredients with your other hand. Knead only long enough to form a firm ball.

Pinch off dough in pieces the size of a lemon, form into ball, and roll out in thin circles on floured board. Cook on hot griddle or in frying pan—no oil on griddle or pan. When tortilla begins to brown, turn and cook on other side. Do not stack these tortillas on top of one another as you cook them, because they tend to steam. Spread them out until they are only warm to the touch and then stack them on a clean dish towel. Cover with another towel and put in warm place until ready to be eaten.

They can be eaten as they are—after all, it's bread—or folded over with various fillings.

FILLINGS

Eggs and Chorizo

Chorizo is a Mexican sausage, pleasantly pepper-hot. They come in links or in bulk form. If in links, remove casings. Crumble it up and fry about five minutes. Remove excess grease from pan. Allow two links to a person. Now, beat up eggs, two to a person, and add to chorizo. Cook until eggs are done. Serve this in folded-over flour tortilla with hot sauce. Good for breakfast, lunch, or dinner.

Beans

For a quick, standup snack, you can't beat some hot frijoles—pinto beans—in a flour tortilla with plenty of hot sauce.

Eggs and Potatoes

Cube cold boiled potatoes. Beat up eggs, allowing at least two per person. In a frying pan with about two tablespoons bacon drippings, cook potatoes until they begin to brown and then add beaten up eggs and cook until done. Into the flour tortilla with it!

Eggs, Potatoes and Chorizo

First, fry chorizo. Drain off excess grease, then add cubed boiled potatoes and cook them until almost brown, then add the eggs, cooking until done. Put this in flour tortillas and serve with hot sauce.

Chicken

Shred or cut up cooked chicken that has been boned and skinned. Put chicken in a few tablespoons of chicken broth and add to it about one-half medium-size onion, chopped, some celery, chopped fine, and about one teaspoon Chiliquik. Cook a few minutes or until liquid has practically cooked away. Put serving into flour tortilla and fold over.

All of these flour tortilla sandwiches consisting of chorizo, eggs, etc., make a good meal, especially with a goodly helping of refried beans.

Enchiladas

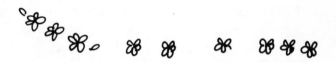

During World War II, a group of us in San Francisco, all displaced Texans, became frantic for Mexican food, Texas style. Although none of us at that time knew beans about cooking, we finally succeeded in rounding up the necessary ingredients and made some enchiladas. I suppose they were pretty bad, but we happily devoured them and proclaimed them equal to nectar of the gods.

CHEESE ENCHILADAS

4 tablespoons flour
¼ cup cooking oil
2 tablespoons chili powder
2 teaspoons cumin
1 teaspoon salt
2 cloves garlic, crushed
2 ⅔ cups hot water
10 oz. cheddar cheese, grated
10 tortillas (preferably red)
1 medium onion, chopped

Brown flour in oven until golden brown. In frying pan with cooking oil, put browned flour, chili powder, cumin, garlic, and salt. Blend well. Over low fire, gradually add water, stirring constantly. If flour begins to lump, remove from fire immediately and stir until lumps are gone. Then place over fire again and continue adding water, little by little. Simmer gently for about one hour, stirring occasionally.

While the sauce is cooking, in a small frying pan with one-half inch of cooking oil, hot but not smoking, immerse tortilla for about thirty seconds, turning once. Remove at once with food turner. Tortilla must not get crisp and must remain pliable. Continue until all tortillas have been cooked and put aside in warm place.

An assembly line should now be set up, consisting of about ten ounces grated cheddar cheese, or Mexican-style cheese; one medium onion, chopped; the tortillas; and a shallow baking pan, large enough to hold the ten enchiladas snugly. Or, you can use two pie pans if there's nothing else available.

Place about three heaping tablespoons of cheese along center of tortilla. Add one teaspoon onion, roll up tortilla, and put in pan with the folded side down. Over the rolled up enchiladas, which have been placed close together, pour very hot enchilada sauce. On top of these, sprinkle a little cheese and place in oven that has been heated to 200 degrees and turned off. Leave in oven for about twenty minutes. If you leave the oven on, the cheese melts too much and the enchilada loses its shape. Serve immediately, one or two to a serving.

The enchilada sauce can be made with chile pods which would replace the chili powder used in the regular enchilada recipe. You need about eight chile pods which have been simmered in water for about twenty minutes. Remove from water, remove stems and put through food mill so that skin and seeds are removed. The pulp can then be used in place of the chili powder. These chile pods are not readily obtained everywhere and, believe me, with the chili powder you can make a mean enchilada. Incidentally, enchilada sauce freezes beautifully.

MEAT ENCHILADAS

1 lb. ground chuck
1 teaspoon cumin, ground
2 cloves garlic, crushed
1 teaspoon salt
Pepper to taste
1 small tomato, chopped fine
2 tablespoons water
Cheddar cheese, grated
1 small onion, chopped

In large frying pan (do not use any oil), crumble ground meat, preferably chuck, and cook over a high fire, breaking up meat with fork if necessary, until meat has lost its color and almost all liquid has boiled away. Do not brown meat. Turn fire lower and add garlic, cumin, salt, pepper, tomato, and about two tablespoons water. Cover and cook over very low fire for about twenty minutes. When the meat has finished cooking, it should be quite moist. To achieve this result you may have to add a little water during the cooking time.

Prepare ten tortillas the same as you do for cheese enchiladas. Grate some cheddar cheese and chop up one small onion. You are now ready to assemble.

Place about two heaping tablespoons of meat along center of tortilla. Roll up tortilla and put in pan with the folded side down. Over the rolled up enchiladas, which have been placed close together, pour very hot enchilada sauce (see Cheese Enchiladas for recipe). Top with any meat left over, chopped onions, and a goodly amount of grated cheddar cheese. Place in oven at 350 degrees for about twenty minutes and serve immediately. Very good and very filling. Serves five—two enchiladas to a serving.

CHILI ENCHILADAS

Make regular cheese enchiladas, top with hot chili con carne, and heat in oven.

CHICKEN ENCHILADAS

1 small onion, chopped
1 clove garlic, crushed
1 tablespoon oil
1 can (13 ¾ oz.) chicken broth
3 tablespoons Chiliquik
2 tablespoons flour
Cooking oil
8 red tortillas
2 chicken breasts, cooked
About 4 oz. cheddar cheese, grated

Sauté onion and garlic in oil until onion is clear; gradually add flour, and cook, stirring constantly, until flour has browned slightly; then add Chiliquik and chicken broth. Simmer for about ten minutes.

While the sauce is cooking, immerse tortillas in hot cooking oil for thirty seconds, turning once, and remove immediately with food turner. Do not allow tortilla to get crisp. It must be pliable.

After you have removed bone and skin from chicken breasts, break up chicken meat into rather small pieces. In the center of the tortilla place some chicken and top with about two tablespoons grated cheese and a sprinkling of onion. Fold over the tortilla. Put enchiladas folded side down and close together in shallow pan and pour hot sauce over them. Place in oven which has been heated to 200 degrees and then turned off. Leave them about twenty minutes and serve two to a person.

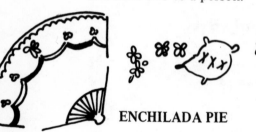

ENCHILADA PIE

Enchilada Pie is a casserole version of enchiladas. I suspect the recipe originated in restaurants in order that they might use the enchiladas left in the kitchen at the end of the day. By chopping them up, adding more sauce, cheese, and onions, and making them into a casserole dish, they could be served the following day.

The tortillas are prepared as they are for regular enchiladas, i.e., put in hot cooking oil for thirty seconds, etc. Then, for this dish, quarter the tortillas.

Place a layer of cooked tortillas across bottom of casserole, then add a generous layer of grated cheese, sprinkle with a few chopped onions, and pour hot enchilada sauce over it. Repeat until you have enough to feed your group. Heat in oven until hot and serve. This same dish can be made with cooked chicken or meat added.

GREEN ENCHILADAS

These green enchiladas have a delicate flavor and can be dressed up or down pepperwise. They are not as well known as other Mexican dishes and, to my amazement, are not even on the menu of many restaurants here. This recipe makes about twelve to sixteen enchiladas and should be served two to a person unless you are having several dishes.

4 chicken breasts
Salted water
1 celery stalk
½ bay leaf
3 lbs. green tomatoes
4 chiles serranos
Salt to taste
 1 medium onion, chopped
1 clove garlic, crushed
1 tablespoon cooking oil
12 to 16 tortillas
Parmesan or Mexican-style cheese, grated
½ pint sour cream

Simmer chicken breasts in salted water with a piece of celery and one-half bay leaf until done. Remove skin and bones from chicken and shred into medium-size pieces. Set aside in warm place with a few spoonfuls of the liquid to keep the chicken moist.

Boil tomatoes and hot peppers in water to cover for ten minutes. Remove from water. Peel tomatoes and crush with peppers. Do *not* put in blender and do *not* remove seeds—you want the mixture to remain pulpy looking. Add salt to taste.

Sauté onions and garlic in small amount of cooking oil and add to tomato mixture. Set aside.

Heat cooking oil, about one-half inch deep, in frying pan until hot but not smoking. Immerse tortilla for about thirty seconds, turning it once, and remove with food turner immediately. Tortilla must not get at all crisp and should remain pliable. Continue until all tortillas are cooked.

Place some chicken in center of tortilla and roll up to look like a fat cigar. Put in shallow pan, folded edge down. Continue until all chicken and tortillas are used. Over the rolled up enchiladas, which have been placed close to one another, put heated tomato mixture, sprinkle with cheese, and top with dollops of sour cream. Put under broiler for about five to seven minutes and serve immediately. The tomato sauce freezes well.

Main Course Dishes

ARROZ CON POLLO

This is an excellent party dish as it can be cooked and left in a warm oven for thirty to forty-five minutes while you socialize with your guests. It is a meal in itself and only a salad need be added.

1 fryer, cut up
4 or 5 chicken breasts
1 ½ cups rice
1 medium onion, chopped
Cooking oil
1 clove garlic, crushed
1 bay leaf
¾ teaspoon sweet basil
2 teaspoons salt
Pepper to taste
1 can (14 ¾ oz.) chicken broth
1 can (14 ½ oz.) tomatoes, broken up
1 fresh tomato, chopped fine
1 box mushrooms, sautéed, or
2 small cans mushrooms
¾ cup dry Marsala
1 package frozen peas
1 medium-sized can pimientos, chopped

Use a large, deep saucepan for this recipe. Pat chicken pieces dry with paper towels, and fry in about one-half inch cooking oil until browned and well done. Remove from pan. Pour off and reserve about half the oil and sauté onion, garlic, bay leaf and sweet basil; add salt and pepper. Sauté until onion is clear.

Add chicken, chicken broth, tomatoes, canned or fresh mushrooms, and Marsala. Cook about thirty minutes, slowly.

Sauté rice in leftover oil and add it, the peas, and the pimientos to chicken. Cook twenty minutes or until rice is done. Do not stir or cook too long or rice will become mushy. Serves six or seven.

ANTICUCHOS

5 lbs. beef filet, cut in 2-inch squares
1 cup, 2 oz. wine vinegar
8 oz. water
2 teaspoons salt
½ teaspoon black pepper
2 garlic cloves, crushed
4 chiles serranos, chopped find
¾ oz. ground oregano

Put chiles with some of the water in blender until it makes a paste. In large bowl (not metal) put pepper and water paste and all other ingredients. Marinate eight to ten hours. Meat must be covered by liquid, and if it isn't, turn it every two hours.

Remove meat from marinade and put on skewers, about six or eight pieces to a skewer. Squeeze onion juice over meat and cook over charcoal fire, basting meat periodically with marinade mixture. Serves five.

This is a shish kebob similar to that served in Night in Old San Antonio, an annual event put on during Fiesta Week in San Antonio, and it is easily the most popular item served.

CHILI CON CARNE

Chili con carne is the granddaddy of them all when it comes to Mexican food à la Texas. I have been told that it isn't Mexican any more than chop suey is Chinese. Recipes for chili are jealously guarded and the city folk scream about the authenticity of the recipe—the country folk just cook it and eat it. H. Allen Smith and Wick Fowler are cases in point. Each one loudly claims that his chili is the best. They proceed with an elaborate ritual, demanding that one use only primitive methods. Long hours are spent over the wood stove, strange encantations are spoken, and, I suspect, a bit of elbow bending takes place. Silly men! They are enjoying themselves, but are not making the best chili in the world. In less than two hours and with ingredients from the supermarket, I, and many other housewives, can outcook them any day of the week.

2 lbs. chuck, ground for chili
4 tablespoons bacon grease
2 large onions, chopped
5 large cloves garlic, crushed
2 teaspoons salt
2 teaspoons ground cumin
4 well rounded tablespoons Chiliquik
4 tablespoons chili powder
Water

Sauté meat in bacon drippings, only until meat turns color and water from meat has evaporated. Add onion and garlic and sauté until onion is clear. Add salt, cumin, Chiliquik and chili powder and stir until thoroughly blended. Then add barely enough water to cover meat, bring to boil, turn fire very low, cover, and cook about one hour or until meat is tender. Check occasionally to see that there is sufficient liquid. It may be necessary to add a little water if the meat begins to stick. After meat is cooked, remove excess fat with baster, add to meat about one heaping tablespoon cornstarch, dissolved in a little water, and cook a few more minutes until mixture is thickened. The chili should resemble meat in a rather thick gravy.

This is *muy* hot, so cut down on the chili powder if you're a sissy. Serves four to six people.

This chili can be eaten as is or heaped over tamales, rice or enchiladas. Also, you can add drained cooked pinto beans to the cooked chili and have a one-dish meal.

TAMALES

Cooking tamales, from my viewpoint, is a monumental task and should not be undertaken unless you are in the Himalayas or an equally remote spot and you feel you will perish unless you have a tamale. This horrendous venture takes two days unless you are a speed demon with a highly geared metabolism. However, every self-respecting Mexican family makes dozens of tamales for the Christmas holidays. They have my respect.

First day:

6 lbs. boneless pork
1 ½ lbs. ground chuck
4 tablespoons salt
3 cloves garlic
1 head garlic, cleaned and mashed
2 tablespoons cumin, crushed
1 tablespoon black pepper
8 chili pods (they are wrinkled and either
  black or dark red)
2 tablespoons cooking oil

Cut up pork into three-inch squares. Place in large pot with salt, garlic and enough water to come about two inches above meat. Boil slowly for at least two hours and until tender. Cool until it can be easily handled. Remove from meat broth and put meat through large blade of meat grinder. Save broth. Put aside ground pork.

In frying pan, sauté ground chuck until it turns color. Set aside.

Remove stems from chili pods and wash inside of pods in order to remove seeds. Put in two cups of water, bring to boil and simmer for fifteen minutes. Save water and put pods through food mill or, if you do it by hand, remove thin skin and mash well with fork. Combine chili pod pulp with mashed garlic, cumin, and black pepper, and blend well.

Combine ground pork, ground beef, the mixture of chili pod pulp and spices, one-fourth cup water from chili pods, two tablespoons cooking oil, two tablespoons salt, and about three and one-half cups of broth from pork. Bring to simmer and cook ten minutes.

Refrigerate separately: meat mixture, juice from chili pods, and pork broth.

Second day:

Soak corn shucks in water until softened. Buy masa same day it is used, as it spoils easily. Buy eight and one-half pounds masa. Buy enough shucks to make ten dozen.

Preparation of masa: to make it easier to handle, prepare only half of the masa at a time. To approximately four and one-fourth pounds masa (half of what you have), add one-half pound of pure lard, about two tablespoons of salt, or to taste, and less than one-fourth cup chili pod juice. Using both hands (there is no home mixer that can handle this heavy dough), squeeze mixture, occasionally turning it, until it is well blended. When mixture is sufficiently blended, the dough will not adhere to the back of the hand when the hand is pressed into the dough.

Remove meat from refrigerator and heat until it is warm. Drain shucks. You're ready actually to make the tamales. Here in Texas, we have what we call tamale cans that measure from one and one-half to two feet in height. This is so you can have an idea of the size pot you need. In the event you do not have anything larger than a Dutch oven, do not lose heart. What won't fit can be frozen, about a dozen to each baggie. Raw tamales freeze beautifully. And while we're on the subject of freezing, if you have more meat than masa and shucks, the meat will also freeze.

Cover the bottom of the pot with corn shucks so that tamales will not touch the bottom and run the risk of scorching. In the middle of the bottom, place a cup or bowl of similar size (not plastic). You will lean your tamales against this so that it will resemble a campfire. At this point, if you like your tamales a bit pepper-hot throw into the pot a package of chile petines.

Since the corn shucks may not be wide enough to make a tamale, you might have to use two, overlapping them. They should be about six to eight inches wide. Laying the shucks on your left hand, spread on the masa thinly with a knife. The masa should cover at least half the shuck lengthwise and three-fourths of the shuck in width. When you have done this, place about two teaspoons of the meat in a wiener-like roll the length of the masa. Fold the sides of the shuck toward the middle, letting them overlap, and then fold over the two ends. Place the tamale, folded side down, against the cup or bowl in the pan and place succeeding tamales so that it resembles a campfire. When pot is about three-fourths full of tamales, fill pot half full with water. Cover with clean, wet dish towel, bringing it to edges of pot. Cover with lid, but not tightly. Bring to boil and then turn down flame so that water simmers. Cook about forty-five minutes. To test "doneness" of tamale, lift edge of shuck and if masa separates from shuck, the tamale is done. Makes about ten dozen tamales.

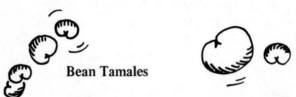

Bean Tamales

Instead of meat, the tamale is filled with beans, which are prepared as follows:

Follow directions for cooking pinto beans. When they are well done, drain and mash. They should be rather dry. Add chile petines and chili powder, which have been blended, and mix well. The chiles and chili powder are added according to the individual taste as some people prefer more peppers than others.

Proceed with tamales, using the bean mixture for the filling.

Chicken Tamales

The same procedure is used as for bean tamales, but substitute cooked, shredded chicken instead of beans.

CHILES RELLENOS

Chiles rellenos are truly delicious and a marvelous company dish. I am defeated by this recipe, however. When I finish cooking it, my kitchen is a shambles and there seem to be egg whites and flour everywhere except on the ceiling. For one thing, the meat keeps falling out of the pepper, and when I finally stand with a dripping, quivering blob on the spoon and think, "This goes into the *frying pan?*" it is a traumatic moment. Also, turning the blob during its cooking time isn't exactly easy, but it all seems worth it when you see them eaten with such gusto. Thank heavens, these can be cooked about forty-five minutes ahead of time if you have a warm place to keep them. This gives you time to restring your nerves.

Tomato Sauce

1 small onion, chopped fine
1 clove garlic
1 tablespoon cooking oil
1 can (14½ oz.) tomato sauce
Pinch sugar
Salt to taste

Sauté onion and garlic, crushed, in cooking oil until onion is clear. Add tomato sauce, a pinch of sugar, and salt to taste. Simmer about ten minutes. Set aside.

1 lb. ground beef
½ medium onion, chopped
1 clove garlic, crushed
½ teaspoon cumin, ground
1 teaspoon salt
1 small tomato, chopped fine
8 chiles poblanos (see Chapter 1 re other
    peppers used)
4 eggs
Cooking oil

Sauté meat until it turns color, add onion, garlic, cumin, and salt, and sauté until onion is clear. Add tomato and simmer about ten minutes. Keep in warm place. A few raisins, parboiled, can be used in the meat mixture if you wish.

Chiles poblanos can be bought canned, and they have been roasted and skinned. On the can they are called green chilies. However, if you can find the fresh ones, the results will be even better. For fresh chiles, roast over flame until skin is split and curled. Remove skin from chiles. Split each chile down the side and remove all seeds, as they are unbelievably hot. Fill peppers with meat filling and roll in flour. Have ready about one-half inch of cooking oil in frying pan.

Separate eggs, beat whites stiff and then beat yellows until lemon colored. Fold egg yolks into egg whites.

Put stuffed, floured chile on large slotted spoon and immerse into egg mixture until chile is covered with egg; then ease into frying pan with hot, but not smoking, oil. Over medium fire cook to a golden brown on all sides and remove to serving plate. Continue with the remainder of the stuffed peppers. Serve with some hot tomato sauce by the side of the chiles rellenos.

CHICKEN MOLE

Chicken breasts, one to a serving
Salt to taste
1 or 2 garlic cloves, crushed
½ teaspoon black pepper
2 tablespoons Doña María Mole*
2 teaspoons cornstarch

Cook chicken in water to cover with garlic, salt, and black pepper until chicken is done— about forty-five minutes. Save broth.

Bone and shred chicken in large pieces. Set aside, keeping warm. In about one and one-half cups of chicken broth, dissolve two tablespoons mole, adding salt to taste and some sugar if you

---

* Mole is a dark brown sauce with a slight chocolate flavor. It is considered quite a delicacy.

so desire. Dissolve cornstarch in small amount of cold water and add to simmering broth until mixture is slightly thickened. Pour over chicken and serve.

CABRITO

March is the month for cabrito (baby goat), when the goats are still young. Found at meat markets in Mexican-American neighborhoods and, perhaps, some supermarkets, all of it is cooked, with the exception of its head and legs.

Cut cabrito into serving-size pieces; salt, pepper, and fry until brown on all sides. Boil in water to cover until tender. Drain and put pieces on individual serving dishes. Top with the following sauce:

1 can (14 ½ oz.) tomatoes, chopped
½ onion, medium, chopped
1 tablespoon cooking oil
½ teaspoon cumin
¼ teaspoon black pepper

Sauté onion and spices in oil; add tomatoes and one-half cup water and boil one minute. Spoon over cabrito. Serve with salad and Mexican rice.

TOMATO AND GUACAMOLE SALAD

On lettuce leaf put two slices of tomato. Top with a glob of guacamole. Stick two or three toasted tortilla triangles into guacamole.

MEXICAN RICE

This recipe is indispensable. Rice can be served with everything in this book except Arroz con Pollo, which has its own rice.

> *2 tablespoons cooking oil*
> *1 cup rice*
> *1 clove garlic, crushed*
> *½ small onion, finely grated*
> *1 teaspoon salt*
> *½ teaspoon cumin, powdered*
> *⅓ 8-oz. can tomato sauce*
> *2 cups water*

Sauté rice in cooking oil until golden. Be careful or it will burn. Add garlic and onion and sauté until onion is clear. Add salt, cumin, tomato sauce and water. Bring to a boil and then simmer for twenty-five to thirty minutes or until rice is done and rather dry. Do not stir or you will have mushy rice.

Mex - Tex Food

GORDITAS

If you cannot find masa, you may use masa harina, following directions on package for making dough.

Make a ball of masa the size of a small egg, only round. Roll into a circle about one-fourth inch thick. In hot, lightly greased frying pan, cook about three minutes on each side, using egg turner to flip over. Crimp edges so it will contain filling. (Keep dipping fingers in cold water as you crimp, as gorditas are quite hot.) Fill with taco meat topped with grated cheese or with chicken as prepared for tacos. Slip egg turner under gorditas and slide onto greasd cookie sheet. Bake at 250 degrees for fifteen minutes. Top with hot sauce or chopped lettuce and tomatoes.

CALABACITAS

1 lb. lean pork, cubed
½ medium onion, chopped
½ teaspoon cumin, crushed
1 teaspoon salt
  teaspoon black pepper
2 chiles serranos, chopped
3 calabacitas, cut up and seeded
3 tomatoes, seeded and chopped

Fry pork until browned. Drain off excess grease and sauté onion with meat until onion is clear. Add other ingredients, cover and cook about forty-five minutes or until calabacitas are done. For the uninitiated, calabacitas are Mexican squash.

CHILEQUILES

6 to 8 tortillas
Bacon grease
½ medium onion, chopped
1 can (8 oz.) tomatoes, cut up, with juice
½ teaspoon salt
1 clove garlic, crushed
1 or 2 chiles serranos (optional)
1 cup grated cheese, goat cheese or
*   Mexican-style cheese*

Stale tortillas are in order for this dish. If necessary, leave them out until they are dry and leathery. Cut each tortilla in about six pieces and cook until crisp in hot bacon drippings, using as little grease as possible.

Sauté onion until clear. Remove excess grease. Put tortillas in with onions and add tomatoes, salt, garlic, and chiles serranos which have been cut up fine. Cook two or three minutes. Sprinkle cheese over all, turn fire off, cover and leave for a few minutes before serving so that cheese is melted.

Goat's cheese or Mexican-style cheese can be used instead of the regular cheese. It is crumbled over chilequiles just before serving.

This makes a good breakfast dish and is often served with a fried egg on top. As with huevos rancheros, refried beans go well.

RAJAS

Rajas should be made from chiles poblanos to have the authentic flavor, but they are also good with bell peppers or Anaheim peppers. The latter two should be parboiled before using.

6 chiles poblanos, peeled and sliced
6 medium onions, parboiled and sliced
2 cloves garlic, mashed
2 tablespoons cooking oil

Chiles poblanos are available either in cans (labelled "green chilies") or fresh. The fresh ones will give you better results. For preparation of fresh chiles poblanos, see instructions under Chiles Rellenos on page 72. Parboil sliced onions and drain on paper towels. You should have equal amounts of chiles and onions. Fry chiles and onions with garlic in cooking oil. Cook until they are soft, and salt according to taste. Do not brown. Drain on paper towels and serve hot.

This is a good vegetable dish, generally served with Steak Tampequeña.

EMPANADAS, MEXICAN STYLE

This empanada is stuffed with spiced meat and can be used for lunches or late snacks.

> *1 lb. ground beef*
> *1 teaspoon chili powder*
> *½ teaspoon cumin*
> *½ teaspoon black pepper*
> *1 clove garlic, crushed*

Sauté meat until it turns color, add spices, and simmer about ten minutes.

Add one-half teaspoon chili powder to empanada dough as you are making it and proceed as you do for other empanadas using the meat for the filling.

MENUDO

If you are squeamish about what you eat, you might not care for this dish, as it is made with tripe, which is the stomach of a cow. Those courageous souls who try it, however, consider it a delicious dish.

2 lbs. tripe, cut in 1-inch squares
2 to 3 teaspoons salt
1 teaspoon cumin
½ teaspoon black pepper
1 can (14½ oz.) hominy, yellow or white
1 lb. raw pork knuckles
4 cloves garlic, mashed
4 tablespoons chili powder
1 tablespoon oregano
2 tablespoons butter

Wash tripe in hot water and then boil with two to three teaspoons salt in three quarts water for two to three hours or until tripe is tender. In separate saucepan cook one pound pork knuckles for one hour.

In saucepan, blend melted butter, garlic, cumin, black pepper, chili powder, and oregano, and fry two to three minutes. Combine tripe, pork knuckles, broth from both tripe and knuckles, spices and one can hominy, preferably yellow. Boil five minutes. Serve with tortillas. Top menudo with chopped onions and a few drops of lemon juice.

It may be necessary to thicken sauce with a flour and water paste if the sauce is too soupy.

HUEVOS RANCHEROS

This is essentially a breakfast dish, but I will eat it at any time of the day or night. If you have some of the hot tomato sauce already prepared, it is an excellent dish to serve guests for a late evening snack.

1 small onion, chopped
2 cloves garlic, crushed
Bacon grease
2 medium-sized tomatoes, chopped fine
1 teaspoon salt
3 to 4 chilles serranos, chopped fine
Eggs
Tortillas

Sauté onion and garlic in small amount of bacon drippings until onion is clear and beginning to brown. Add tomatoes, hot peppers, and salt, and simmer fifteen minutes. Set aside. This amount is enough for four servings. Larger amounts can be made and refrigerated for about a week.

In another frying pan, heat cooking oil about one-half inch deep until hot but not smoking. Immerse tortilla for about thirty seconds, turning it once, and remove immediately with food turner, and put on warm plate. Tortilla must not get crisp. Continue frying until all tortillas are cooked, using one tortilla for each serving. Then fry one or two eggs for each person, depending upon his or her appetite. Eggs should be cooked sunny side up unless you prefer them otherwise. On each dinner plate place one tortilla. On top of it put egg, or eggs, and over each serving spoon heated tomato sauce. Serve immediately with refried beans. *¡Muy bueno!   ¡Muy caliente!*

CARNE GUIZADO

1 lb. stew meat
2 tablespoons cooking oil
½ 6-oz. can tomato paste
1 can (10 ½ oz.) beef broth (bouillon)
1 teaspoon salt
½ teaspoon black pepper
2 cloves garlic, crushed
1 teaspoon chili powder
½ teaspoon cumin
2 small chiles serranos
¾ cup water

Brown meat in oil until brown on all sides. Pour off grease. Add tomato paste, beef broth, salt and pepper, garlic, chili powder, cumin, chile peppers, and water. Bring to boil and then turn very low, cover, and simmer about one and one-half hours, or until meat is tender.

Dissolve about one teaspoon cornstarch in small amount of cold water and slowly pour into stew, which is simmering, until proper thickness of gravy is obtained. Serve with rice.

STEAK TAMPEQUEÑA

½ cup cooking oil
4 chiles serranos, minced
3 cloves garlic, crushed
Juice of 1 lime
1 teaspoon salt
½ teaspoon pepper
½ teaspoon paprika
1 teaspoon oregano
1 teaspoon chili powder
2 beef tenderloin steaks, cut lengthwise

Mix together all ingredients and marinate steaks in this mixture for several hours.

Drain meat and charcoal broil. Baste with marinade while cooking.

Serve with rajas and refried beans. If you are cooking more than two steaks, you will have to increase amount of marinade mixture.

American Recipes Influenced by Tex-Mex Cooking

HAMBURGER MEXICANA

Broil or charcoal broil one-inch thick ground beef patties, one per serving. Place on serving plate and top with slice of American cheese. Cover with hot pinto beans and top with a few chopped onions. A meal in itself.

JALAPEÑO JELLY

*⅓ cup jalapeño peppers, chopped
and seeded*
¾ cup bell peppers, chopped and seeded
1 ½ cups vinegar
5 ½ cups sugar
1 bottle pectin

Cook peppers, vinegar and sugar ten minutes. Add pectin and boil one minute. Let stand fifteen minutes before putting in jars. Seal with paraffin. Makes six half-pint jars.

CHILI CASSEROLE

Leftover chili con carne can be put to good use in this dish. Children love this concoction, and there's nothing better on a cold winter's day.

In a casserole, put a layer of hot chili con carne (see page 65), a layer of grated yellow cheese, and a layer of Fritos. You may, if you wish, sprinkle on some chopped onion. Repeat this process until you have enough to feed your group. Put in a 350-degree oven and heat until piping hot and until cheese is melted. A good one-dish supper.

TAMALE PIE

This is truly a lazy man's meal because it can be whipped together in no time flat, i.e. if you have left-over chili.

2 cups chili con carne
6 tamales, cut in 1-inch pieces
2 cups corn chips
½ cup chopped onions
1 cup cheddar cheese, grated

Assemble the chili con carne, tamales, corn chips, and chopped onions in a baking dish. Sprinkle cheese over the top and bake in a 350-degree oven for thirty minutes.

CHILE CON QUESO AMERICANO

For those who prefer a bland chile con queso, the following recipe will be satisfactory. This can be used as a dip or part of a meal served over fried tortilla triangles.

2 medium onions, chopped
¼ cup butter
2 4-oz cans green chiles, chopped
  with juice
1 can (14½ oz.) tomatoes, mashed
  a little and drained of juice
18 oz. Monterey Jack cheese, diced in
  ½ -inch pieces
1 cup whipping cream
Fried tortilla triangles
Salt to taste

Sauté onions in butter and add green chilies. Add tomatoes and simmer for about five minutes or until of a thickened quality, which will be thicker than final product. Remove from fire and cool.

Stir into cool mixture cubed cheese and salt to taste. Add one cup whipping cream and stir until uniform. Heat but do not allow to simmer. The purpose is to melt the cheese. Cut in with wooden spoon. Avoid stirring or cheese will aggregate into ball. When cheese is melted, serve over crisp tortilla triangles. Serves about five or six.

ENCHILADAS SAN ANTONIO

½ medium onion, grated
1 clove garlic, crushed
1 tablespoon cooking oil
1 8-oz. can tomato sauce
2 cooked chicken breasts, shredded
1 4-oz. can green chilies
Tortillas
Sour Cream

Sauté onion and garlic in cooking oil until onion is clear. Add tomato sauce and simmer a few minutes. Set aside.

Prepare tortillas—two per serving—as you do for soft tacos. On tortilla place pieces of shredded chicken breast and some cut up green chiles. Roll up and place folded side down on serving plate. Spoon hot tomato sauce over enchiladas and top with sour cream.

Desserts

FLAN

Yes, this is custard, richer than usual and with carmelized sugar. Try it—you'll never go back to whatever you've been cooking.

Carmelize one-half cup sugar in ring mold. Keep turning pan until bottom and lower sides are coated. You can also use a muffin pan if you want individual servings, placing a little sugar in each muffin ring and holding over fire until sugar is carmelized.

2 cups milk
1 cup sugar
½ teaspoon salt
6 beaten eggs
½ teaspoon almond extract

Mix milk, sugar and salt until sugar is dissolved and scald over low fire. Pour these ingredients slowly over the well beaten eggs, beating constantly with electric mixer. Add almond extract. Pour custard into ring or muffin rings, set in pan of water, and bake at 325 degrees for about three-fourths of an hour or until custard is set (when silver knife comes out clean). Chill.

When thoroughly chilled, run knife around edges to loosen. Place serving dish upside down on top of ring mold. Turn both over, holding tightly, and place on table. Shake ring a little and custard will come out. Serves six.

BUNUELOS

4 cups flour
1 teaspoon baking powder
1 teaspoon salt
2 tablespoons sugar
2 eggs, beaten
1 cup milk
¼ cup butter, melted

Sift together dry ingredients. Combine beaten eggs with milk. Fold in dry ingredients and add melted butter. On floured board knead dough as you do for bread.

Make into small balls and roll out to about five inches. Fry in hot fat about one minute on each side. Prick with fork while cooking. Sprinkle with sugar and cinnamon.

POLVORONES

2 cups sifted flour
¾ cup sugar
1 ½ teaspoons cinnamon
1 cup soft butter

Sift together flour, cinnamon and sugar. Cream butter with mixer and gradually add flour mixture. You can use the mixer for about one-half the mixing but you will have to resort to hand mixing for the remainder or run the risk of overheating your mixer.

Pinch off small pieces of dough, form into ball and put on ungreased cookie sheet. Bake at 300 degrees for twenty-five minutes. After baking, sift cinnamon and sugar over cookies.

PRALINES

1 cup dark brown sugar
2 cups white sugar
1 cup buttermilk
2 tablespoons white corn syrup
1 teaspoon soda
1 teaspoon vanilla
1 tablespoon butter
2 cups pecan halves and pieces

Mix first five ingredients in a large saucepan. Soda will cause mixture to foam. Cook, stirring, over medium flame until the mixture reaches the soft ball stage. Remove from fire and add butter, vanilla and pecans. Beat until it begins to harden and becomes glossy. Pour large spoonfuls onto waxed paper.

CAPIROTADA

In case you're wondering, this is Mexican bread pudding. I am including two recipes for this dessert. This one is sweeter than the other recipe.

¾ cup brown sugar
¾ cup water
½ teaspoon cinnamon
6 slices day-old bread, toasted
½ cup peanuts
½ cup raisins
1 banana, cubed
¼ lb. goat or Mexican-type cheese
Pinch salt
1 tablespoon butter

Mix together in saucepan brown sugar, cinnamon and water. Bring to boil and set aside. In casserole, put layer of toast cubes, peanuts, raisins, banana and cheese, cubed. Sprinkle with pinch of salt. Repeat until ingredients are used. Over this pour sugar, water and cinnamon mixture, dot with butter and bake in oven at 350 degrees for twenty minutes. Serve hot or cold with cream.

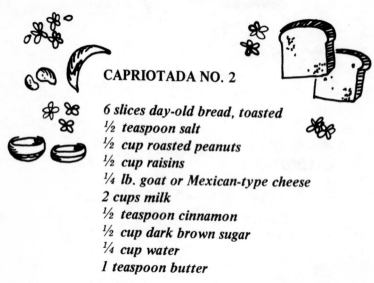

CAPRIOTADA NO. 2

6 slices day-old bread, toasted
½ teaspoon salt
½ cup roasted peanuts
½ cup raisins
¼ lb. goat or Mexican-type cheese
2 cups milk
½ teaspoon cinnamon
½ cup dark brown sugar
¼ cup water
1 teaspoon butter

In casserole, put layer of toast cubes, peanuts, raisins, and cheese, cubed. Sprinkle with salt. Repeat until ingredients are used. Over this pour milk and cinnamon which has been brought to boil in saucepan. Bake twenty minutes in 350-degree oven.

Boil sugar and water together a few minutes and add butter. This can be poured over pudding when served, or the pudding can be served with cream.

Some Typical Menus

BREAKFAST:

Huevos rancheros
Refried beans
Flour tortillas

Chilequiles topped with fried egg
Refried beans

Eggs and chorizo
Hot sauce
Refried beans
Flour tortillas

LUNCH:

Green enchiladas
Salad
Polverones

Chalupas
Guacamole and tomato salad
Flan

Flaquitos with guacamole
Mexican rice
Sherbert

DINNER:

Chiles rellenos
Avocado tacos
Mexican rice
Capirotada

Arroz con pollo
Chile con queso
Tomato and guacamole salad
Flan

Carne asada
Chilequiles with goat cheese
Rajas
Guacamole with crisp tortilla triangles
Refried beans with crisp tortilla triangles

Anticuchos
Mexican rice
Rajas
Flan

"REGULAR" DINNER:

Enchilada
Tamales
Chili
Rice
Beans
Sherbet or Pralines

COCKTAIL PARTY:

Margueritas
Guacamole dip with flaquitos
Chile con queso with corn chips
Empanadas

NOTES

NOTES

NOTES

NOTES

NOTES

NOTES

NOTES

NOTES

NOTES

NOTES